Dealing in cryptocurrency:

A guild to mastering NFTs, potential revenue, and stock marketing.

By

Steven C. Woodard

TABLE OF CONTENT

Introduction

If you consider the most popular asset classes owned by individual investors (stocks, bonds, gold, and real estate), all of them have been existing for more than a century, with the exception of gold and real estate, which date back thousands of existence Certain derivatives of this, such as ETF options and REITS, have been seen, but never a completely new asset class like crypto currencies. Certainly not during my lifetime. Financial fads have existed during my lifetime. The global financial crisis of 2008 was followed by dotcom booms in the late 1990s, and more recently, the emergence of crypto currency. Which brings up the question of where crypto currency fits into the spectrum? Is it a valuable asset that can change your life or just a passing trend in money? Both are the proper responses. With crypto currency, more people than ever will become millionaires.

However, many average investors will lose money and their shirts. It is my hope that you fall into the first category after reading this book.

Chapter 1

How does crypto currency work? What is it?

Several kinds of cash that exists digitally or practically and uses cryptography to maintain transactions is referred to as crypto currency, sometimes known as crypto-currency, or simply as crypto. Cryptocurrencies use a decentralized mechanism to track transactions and create new units rather than a central authority to issue or regulate them.

Crypto currency: What is it?

A digital imbursement scheme recognized as crypto currency doesn't rely on banks to legalize dealings.

Peer-to-peer knowledge makes it likely for anyone, wherever, to send and receive expenditure expenses made by means of crypto currencies do not live as real physical coins that can be ecstatic and exchanged; quite, they only survive as digital entries to an online file that point human being transactions. A free ledger keeps track of all bitcoin transactions so as to engage funds transfer. Digital wallets are wherever crypto currency is held in reserve.

Due to the reality that dealings are established by means of encryption, crypto currency has earned its name. This means that the storage, program, and recording of bitcoin statistics to community ledgers all involve complicated system. Encryption's objective is to present safety and defense.

The initial crypto currency was formed during 2009 plus is still the most famous now: Bitcoin. A great piece of crypto currency concern is in trading for fiscal gain, through speculators rarely sending prices stratospheric.

What is the procedure of crypto currency?

A distributed public ledger known as blockchain, which is updated and maintained by currency holders, is the foundation of crypto currencies.

Through a process known as mining, which employs computer power to solve challenging mathematical problems, units of Bitcoin is created. In addition, users include the choice of purchasing the currencies from brokers, afterward storing and spending them in digital wallets.

When you embrace crypto currencies, you don't really have anything. What you own is a answer that enables you to move a record or a piece of quantity among people lacking the use of a dependable third party.

In spite of the reality that Bitcoin has been accessible since 2009; the financial applications of crypto currencies and blockchain knowledge are continually budding, and extra are expected in the future. The technology may perhaps one day be used to trade bonds, equities, and further financial assets.

Examples of crypto currencies

Many crypto currencies are here. Amongst the well-identified are:

Bitcoin:

The unique crypto currency and still the good number traded, Bitcoin was recognized during 2009.

The individual or set, whose exact uniqueness is still unidentified, typically regarded as a alias Satoshi Nakamoto, is accredited with creating the currency.

Ethereum:

Ethereum, a blockchain proposal formed in 2015, have its own digital currency called Ether (ETH), also known as Ethereum. After Bitcoin, it is the mainly extensively used crypto currency.

Litecoin:

Regardless of moving extra speedily to expand fresh thoughts, such as speedier payments and processes to let more transactions, this money is most equivalent to bitcoin.

Ripple:

A circulated ledger scheme called Ripple was formed in 2012.

Ripple is a means that can be used to track more than just cryptocurrency transactions. The association that formed it has collaborated with frequent banks and financial organizations.

The term "altcoins" is used to differentiate non-Bitcoin crypto currencies from the original.

How to purchase crypto currencies

You might be thinking about secure crypto currency purchases. Classically, there are three steps. Which are:

First step: selecting a platform

Selecting the platform is the first step. Naturally, you have two options: a typical broker or a exact bitcoin exchange:

- Customary brokers. These are online brokers that give customers the option to purchase and sell crypto currencies as well as traditional financial instruments including equities, bonds, and exchange-traded funds (ETFs) though they have smaller amount crypto capabilities, a number of platforms have abridged trading costs.

- Exchanges for crypto currencies. There are many crypto currency connections to choose from, and they all give right of entry to a selection of digital assets, wallet storage, interest-bearing account alternatives, and other features. Asset-based costs are general on exchanges.

When contrasting various platforms, take into account the crypto currencies they support, the fees they levied, the security measures they had in place, the possibilities for storage and withdrawal, and any available educational materials.

Funding your account is step two.

The next step is to finance your bank account so you are able to begin trading after selecting your trading platform even though it differs by platform, the greater part of cryptocurrency exchanges let users purchase cryptocurrency with money(i.e., administration-issued) currencies resembling the US Dollar, the British Pound, or the Euro with their debit or credit cards.

Credit card purchases of cryptocurrencies are frowned ahead, and various exchanges do not support them. quite a few credit card companies as well prohibit cryptocurrency transactions. This is due to the reality with the aim of cryptocurrencies are pretty unpredictable, making it imprudent to danger incurring debt or paying large credit card transaction fees for a few assets. Additionally, certain platforms will accept wire transactions and ACH transfers.

Every platform has a dissimilar set of satisfactory expense options and processing period for deposits and withdrawal. The time it takes for deposits to reconcile also varies depending on the expense category.

Fees are a necessary contemplation. These comprise likely business cost for deposits and withdrawals in addition to trading costs. Fees will differ by payment method and platform, so do your research up front.

Making a purchase

You can place an order using the web or mobile platforms of your broker or exchange. You can purchase cryptocurrencies by clicking "buy," selecting the order type, entering the quantity, and then completing the order if you intend to do so. The comparable technique is used for "sell" orders.

Extra methods of investing in cryptocurrency continue living. These comprises payment platforms that allow clients buy, sell, or keep cryptocurrencies, for instance PayPal, Cash App, and Venmo. The following investment vehicles are also available:

• Bitcoin trusts: Shares of Bitcoin trusts can be purchased using a standard brokerage account. These products offer regular investors access to cryptocurrencies via the stock souk

• Bitcoin shared finances: You are able to decide from Bitcoin ETFs and mutual funds.

• Blockchain companies that specialize in the technology behind cryptocurrency and cryptocurrency transactions are another way to indirectly invest in cryptocurrency through stocks or ETFs.

You can also invest in the stocks or exchange-traded funds (ETFs) of businesses that utilize blockchain technology.

What's best for you will depend on your risk tolerance and investing objectives.

How to keep cryptocurrencies protected

After buying cryptocurrency, you have to store it strongly to stop stealing or hacks. Crypto wallets are typically used to store cryptocurrencies. These physical wallets or online programs are used to securely store your private keys to your cryptocurrencies. Some exchanges allow you store money directly through the site by offering wallet services. However, not all brokers or exchanges will automatically offer you wallet services.

There are many wallet providers from which to choose. "Hot wallet" in addition to "cold wallet" is terms that are used:

- Hot wallet storage: "hot wallets" are a sort of cryptocurrency storage that uses internet software to look after your assets' confidential keys.
- Cold wallet storage: Unlike hot wallets, which make use of online computers to keep your personal keys, cold wallets (at times referred to as hardware wallets) use offline electronic strategy.

What can you obtain with cryptocurrencies?

After it was originally introduced, Bitcoin was destined to be a means for daily transactions, allowing users to purchase anything from a cup of coffee to a computer or even expensive commodities like real estate.

That hasn't yet happened, and although more institutions are beginning to embrace cryptocurrencies, big transactions using them are still uncommon. Despite this, crypto can be used to purchase a wide range of goods through e-commerce platforms. Here are a small number of instances:

Technology as well as online stores

On their websites, an amount of businesses that present tech products allow cryptocurrency, together with newegg.com, AT&T, and Microsoft. A platform for online shopping called Overstock was one of the first to accept Bitcoin. It is furthermore acknowledged by Home Depot, Rakuten, and Shopify.

Expensive goods:

Some upscale stores accept cryptocurrency as payment. For example, Bitdials, an online luxury supermarket, accepts Bitcoin in trade for luxury watches like Rolex, Patek Philippe, along with others.

Cars:

Some auto dealers now accept bitcoin as payment, ranging from high-end luxury dealers to mass-market brands.

Insurance:

AXA, a Swiss insurer, stated in April 2021 that it has started taking Bitcoin as a form of payment for all insurance lines other than life insurance (due to regulatory issues). The US-based home and vehicle insurance broker Premier Shield Insurance also accepts Bitcoin for premium costs

Use a bitcoin debit card, like BitPay in the US, if you wish to spend cryptocurrency at a store that doesn't take it directly.

Scam and frauds connecting cryptocurrencies

Unluckily, there is an amplify in bitcoin criminality. Amongst the cryptocurrency frauds are:

Bogus websites: cheat sites with false reviews and cryptocurrency jargon that promise enormous, guaranteed profits as long as you keep investing.

Virtual Ponzi schemes: Cybercriminals that deal in digital currencies advertise fictitious investment possibilities and give the impression of big profits by paying off previous investors with funds from new investors. Before the perpetrators of one scam, Bit Club Network, were charged in December 2019, they raised more than $700 million.

"Celebrity" endorsements: Online fraudsters make up to be millionaires or famous figures, promising to increase your investment in a virtual currency while really stealing what you give. They might also spread rumors about a well-known businessperson supporting a particular cryptocurrency via messaging applications or chat forums. The scammers sell their stake after they have induced investors to purchase and raised the price, which causes the currency's value to fall.

Scams involving romance: The FBI issues a warning on a surge in online dating scams in which con artists convince victims they meet on dating apps or social media to make investments or transact in virtual currencies. within the first seven months of 2021, the FBI's Internet offense Complaint Center acknowledged over 1,800 information of romance scams by means of a cryptocurrency theme, with losses toting up $133 million.

Otherwise, scammers may set up fake exchanges or assume the identity of actual virtual currency merchants in order to defraud individuals out of their funds fake sales presentations for cryptocurrency-based human being withdrawal plans form yet an additional crypto trick. After that there is plain-vanilla cryptocurrency hacking, in which thieves get information to people's digital wallets wherever they store their virtual money and obtain what they wish for.

Are cryptocurrencies protected?

Blockchain technology is classically used to generate cryptocurrencies. Blockchain explains how transactions are time-stamped in addition to recorded into "blocks." A digital record of bitcoin transactions is created as a result, which is difficult for hackers to alter despite being a pretty complicated, technical procedure.

Business also requires a two-factor confirmation process. To start a contract, for example, you could be required to enter a username and secret word. The next step can entail entering an verification code that was provided to your private telephone using SMS. Even when there are safety actions in place, cryptocurrencies can still be compromised. Cryptocurrency start-ups have been brutally hit by a number of expensive cyber attacks. The two largest cryptocurrency hacks of 2018 involved Coin check, which was targeted for $534 million, and Bit Grail, which was targeted for $195 million.

The worth of effective currencies is completely determined by supply and demand, not like currency assured by the government.

This can lead to unreliable swings that also consequence in huge gains for investors or losses intended for them in addition, compared toward conventional fiscal instruments similar to stocks, bonds, and mutual funds, investments in cryptocurrencies are protected by legislative oversight radically less often.

Four suggestions for safe cryptocurrency investment

All investments have risk, according to Consumer Reports, but some experts think that cryptocurrency is one of the riskier investing options available today. These pointers might assist you in making informed decisions if you intend to invest in cryptocurrency.

Research collaborations

Learn about bitcoin exchanges before making a venture there are thought to be more than 500 exchanges accessible before making a decision, do your homework, study reviews, and consult with more seasoned investors.

Understand how to safely keep your digital currency:

You must store cryptocurrency if you purchase it. You can save it in a digital wallet or on an exchange. Wallets come in a lot of varieties, plus all has advantages, technical requirements, in addition to safety values that should be met. You should research your storage options before investing, just like with exchanges.

Make a variety of investments:

Any sound investment strategy must incorporate diversification, and investing in cryptocurrencies is no exception.

Don't invest all of your funds in Bitcoin, for instance, just because you are familiar with the name. There are countless possibilities, thus it's best to diversify your investments among several currencies.

Be ready for turbulence:

Because of the market's extreme volatility, be ready for ups and downs. There will be substantial changes in price. Cryptocurrency might not be the best option for you if your investment portfolio or mental health can't manage that.

However, keep in mind that cryptocurrency is still in its relative infancy and is regarded as highly speculative. Be ready for challenges while investing in something new. Do your homework and start investing prudently if you intend to take part.

Using a thorough antivirus is one of the best methods to keep secure when browsing the internet. You are protected by Kaspersky Internet Security from malware infections, spyware, data theft, and online payment security utilizing bank-grade encryption.

Chapter 2

Knowledge about the Crypto Ecosystem

Since the creation of Bitcoin during 2009, the cryptocurrency market has expanded rapidly. Initially more of a specialized interest, Bitcoin has grown into a sizable business that includes crypto exchanges, blockchain protocols, financial services, data aggregators, technology suppliers, media, conferences, Smartphone apps, hardware tools, and an evolving regulatory arrangement

Bitcoin exchanges

The most significant part of the crypto economy is undoubtedly the exchanges themselves.

The pricing of the different crypto assets that are now accessible are set by the trading activity that takes place on these exchanges, which operate as the on- and off-ramps for investors and traders moving into and out of the cryptocurrency marketplace

Huge amounts of money being transferred through cryptocurrency exchanges, with the top 5 reporting an average daily transaction of over $3 billion, according to **CoinMarketCap.**

There are hundreds of cryptocurrency exchanges operating globally, some of which target the general public, and others of which concentrate on specialized markets.

By integrating the crypto ecosystem to the global economy and employing LSEG Technology's matching engine to deliver best-in-class technological capability unmatched by any other crypto exchange, AAX, for instance, targets institutional investors and traders of cryptocurrencies.

What they all have in common is that they created the foundation for several alternative coins that have successfully captured market share years after their release. Crypto no longer refers just to Bitcoin. Other coins, including ETH, XRP, BCH, USDT, LTC, EOS, XTZ, and others, all have a place in the portfolios and diversification plans of many cryptocurrency traders.

With all these markets, trading cryptocurrency now resembles forex trading greatly because the same underlying ideas, resources, instruments, and tactics utilized in forex trading also apply to trading cryptocurrency. In the crypto trading part of AAX Academy, we go through these issues in great detail. Common indications include Elliot Wave, Stochastic, CCI, Inside Bar Breakout, and Cup and Handle.

Cryptocurrency protocols

Blockchain is the underlying technology that enables cryptocurrencies. Blockchain protocols come in a wide variety, each with slightly unique technological characteristics, advantages, and disadvantages. One blockchain might not have mining at all and instead employ Delegated Proof of Stake, whereas the Bitcoin blockchain, for instance, relies on mining and Delegated Proof of Work to process transactions.

Other noteworthy protocols include ETH, Hyperledger, EOS, XLM, IOST, KIN, TRX, and STEEM in addition to the Bitcoin blockchain. Ethereum merits special recognition among all of these blockchain protocols for fostering quick innovation across the whole crypto business

The Ethereum platform, developed by Vitalik Buterin, introduced a more open market for developers using its own programming language Solidity. It revolutionized blockchain technology and ushered in a new era of cutting-edge decentralized applications enabled by smart contracts and unique tokens (the majority of altcoins in use today are based on the ERC20 standard for Ethereum).

The Ethereum blockchain system serves as the foundation for the decentralized finance movement, also known as DeFi.

Monetary services

Every service that is offered in conventional finance has an accessible equivalent in DeFi apps built on Ethereum. DeFi apps give users the ability to do a variety of things, including mint stablecoins, make and receive payments, take out loans, trade, participate in prediction markets, invest in real estate, and much more. Decentralized services are only possible because to smart contracts, which automatically carry out pre-agreed actions if certain conditions are satisfied.

However, conventional finance has now changed to provide new services designed for the cryptocurrency economy.

Custodians offer security services to those who have a significant amount of money invested in cryptocurrencies, some fund managers now give investors a way to include cryptocurrencies in their portfolios, and many analysts on mainstream media, like Bloomberg, are now seriously interested in cryptocurrencies.

Bitcoin hardware

There is a sizable crypto hardware market that provides long-term HODLers and professional traders with the resources they require for people who like to take security precautions into their own hands. Trezor and Ledger are the two most well-known brands in the hard wallet market. Both effectively provide crypto traders with the same benefit: a location to keep cryptocurrency in a method that is significantly safer.

Crypto traders generally divide their reserves between hard wallets and an exchange adopting a ratio that suits their trading strategy since cryptocurrency saved in hard wallets is obviously unavailable for trading on the marketplaces.

Analytics using blockchain and data aggregators

Due to the massive quantity of activity occurring across blockchains, a sub-industry of data aggregators and blockchain analytics has emerged in the cryptocurrency ecosystem. The best places to turn to for a quick stats check on cryptocurrencies and exchanges are businesses like CoinMarketCap. They gather information on market cap, trading volume, liquidity, price movement, circulating supply, and industry-wide statistics like the total number of coins, markets, and market capitalization as well as information on BTC's supremacy.

Websites like Blocktivity provide blockchain metrics for individuals who are more interested in that. You can see data for each individual blockchain protocol here, including the number of operations in the previous 24 hours, the average number of operations over the previous week, market capitalization, and the Capacity Utilization Index (CUI), which shows how much of the protocol's total capacity is still available after current actual usage. Together, these websites can offer insightful information about the blockchain production

For instance, EOS is running at just under 50% CUI with an average of 63 million operations over the past seven days, whereas Ethereum's CUI is just over 50% with an average of 667,000 operations. Technically speaking, the EOS protocol outperforms its Ethereum equivalent by a wide margin.

That hasn't stopped Ethereum, meanwhile, from controlling 70% of the market capitalization across the busiest blockchains.

Crypto conferences and media

No industry this large could operate without its own media sector in the digital age, where everyone is essentially a content publisher. A massive media landscape of publications, key opinion leaders, and conferences devoted to the coin, the chain, and the code has arisen from the cryptocurrency business.

Among the top publications covering cryptocurrency news are Coindesk, Cointelegraph, Bitcoin Magazine, Decrypt, CCN, Bitcoinist, NewsBTC, and many others. Some KOLs have achieved enormous success and occasionally have larger audiences than the news media.

Cryptocurrency rules

Financial authorities are, for the most part, still working on the frameworks necessary to safeguard investors and consumers as the crypto ecosystem expands to more individuals in more markets. For businesses that operate in several different jurisdictions, the method authorities take can range greatly.

Many initiatives started during the ICO craze of 2017 and 2018 before the regulatory framework was established, and some projects were abandoned in the middle of the fundraising process because they did not comply with the rules of that jurisdiction once they were made obtainable This was entirely related to the changing understanding of how to categorize digital assets, which is how the distinction between security tokens and utility tokens came to exist.

This push for regulation has gotten stronger over the past year with the Libra proposal, and more and more studies are also coming in from Central Banks as they investigate what blockchain technology could entail for their policies and economic operations.

The cryptocurrency ecosystem is quickly changing.

The various elements that make up the crypto ecosystem are all expanding and changing at their own rates, helping to build an increasingly complex zone from its specialized appeal during 2009 to a thriving digital assets market, cryptocurrency has gone a long way.

But more than a robust ecosystem is required if the sector is to grow and attract more participants. A stronger link between cryptocurrency and international finance is required.

The more familiarity traditional banking and cryptocurrencies have with one another, the simpler it will be for newcomers to begin their grasp of the ecosystem. With each newcomer, the cryptocurrency market also develops further as exchanges, financial services, media, and authorities adapt to the expectations of mainstream consumers, perhaps leading to better investment results.

Chapter 3

The Prospects for Bitcoin in the Second Half of 2022

The crypto market has had a terrible first half of 2022.

Since their all-time highs in late 2021, the price of bitcoin and Ethereum has fallen by more than 50%. Despite some minor gains in recent weeks, the cryptocurrency market as a whole is mainly stagnant. Although no one can be certain, several experts believe that before a sustainable rebound, cryptocurrency values may fall considerably further. In 2021, Bitcoin prices reached a number of new records before seeing sharp dips and increased institutional investment from major corporations. Late last year, Ethereum, the second-largest cryptocurrency, reached its own new record high as well.

However, in June, it fell below $900, its lowest point since the beginning of 2021. The Biden government and U.S. management representatives have shown an increasing interest in new cryptocurrency legislation. People continue to be interested in cryptocurrency, and it has become a hot topic in popular culture gratitude to everybody from experienced investors like Elon Musk to that Facebook buddy from high school. The year 2021 marked a breakthrough in many respects. Long-term forecasting is challenging, but in the near future, industry professionals will be watching developments like institutional acceptance of cryptocurrency payments and regulation to try and gain a better understanding of the business.

Expect ongoing discussions on cryptocurrency regulation as lawmakers in Washington, D.C., and throughout the world attempt to develop rules and laws that will make bitcoin safer for investors and less desirable to hackers. U.S. government representatives have expressed a strong interest in stable coin regulation, particularly in light of the most recent Terra Luna crash. The stable coin TerraUSD (UST) depegged from the dollar in May as a result of the collapse in cryptocurrency markets, which also brought about a drop in the associated cryptocurrency Luna. As a result, many investors from Terra and Luna saw their money disappear within a short period of time. Within a few weeks of Terra's failure, the cryptocurrency market crashed once more. As a result of the dire market conditions, several crypto firms announced layoffs and blocked withdrawals in an effort to reduce costs.

Since then, some businesses have declared bankruptcy, including Celsius and Three Arrows Capital.

Because of the snowball effect, federal officials have suddenly had greater ammunition to advocate for crypto regulation. It is obvious that strict regulation may be coming soon in the wake of the disastrous events that have occurred in the cryptocurrency market over the past several weeks. The failure of DeFi lenders may be the impetus behind regulators' efforts to impose strict regulations on cryptocurrencies. Even though there is still more to be done, there have been significant regulatory advancements in 2022. The "responsible development" of digital assets, including stablecoins, is the subject of an executive order that President Joe Biden signed in March and directed federal departments to examine The first framework resulting from President Biden's executive order on digital assets was just released by the U.S.

Treasury Department. It describes how the U.S. should interact with foreign nations over digital assets. Jerome Powell, the chairman of the Federal Reserve, stated in 2021 that he had "no intention" of outlawing cryptocurrencies in the United States, while Gary Gensler, the chairman of the Securities and Exchange Commission, has frequently discussed the roles played by both his own organization and the Commodity Futures Trading.

Commission in regulating the segment

Gensler has stated on numerous occasions that if tougher regulation is not put in place, investors are likely to suffer. Additionally, it stands to reason that the IRS would want to ensure that investors understand how to disclose virtual money on their tax returns. The remarks of Powell and Gensler are in line with a growing consensus among U.S. politicians and the Biden administration that further regulation of cryptocurrencies is required.

More generally, investor protection around these many service providers, such as the exchanges, lending platforms, and broker-dealers, would be advantageous for the general public at this time. Regulation in the cryptocurrency world faces challenges, as do most things. There are various organizations that might or might not have the authority to oversee things. Since U.S. businesses and investors are now operating without clear standards, unambiguous regulation would mean the removal of a huge obstacle for cryptocurrencies.

Potential effects of new regulations on investors

Although the idea of cryptocurrency regulation can be contentious, many experts believe it will be beneficial to both investors and the sector as total

Increased regulation may lead to greater stability in the famously unstable cryptocurrency market.

As long as it hits the appropriate balance, it may also serve to safeguard long-term investors, stop fraudulent conduct inside the crypto ecosystem, and offer clear guidelines to encourage business innovation in the sector.

Reasonable regulation benefits everyone. It increases people's trust in cryptocurrencies, but I believe we need to take our time and do it properly. In already unpredictable markets, regulatory news may have an impact on cryptocurrency prices. Due to market volatility, experts advise limiting your cryptocurrency investments to no more than 5% of your whole portfolio and never putting money at risk.

Increasing Institutional Cryptocurrency Use

In 2021, mainstream businesses from several sectors showed interest in cryptocurrencies and blockchain technology, and in some cases, they even made their own investments. For instance, AMC declared last year that it would take Bitcoin as payment. By enabling customers to purchase on their platforms, fintech businesses like PayPal and Square are also placing a bet on cryptocurrencies. Despite the fact that the corporation has billions of dollars' worth of cryptocurrency assets, Tesla accepts Dogecoin payments and is still undecided about accepting bitcoin expenses Experts anticipating an enhance in this buy-in.

We've seen a massive influx of interest, and that will continue to fuel the industry's expansion for some time to come.

What increased adoption by institutions means for investors

While most individuals don't currently see the benefit of purchasing with cryptocurrencies, as more merchants begin to accept them, the situation may change. even though it might receive a short time before buying goods or services by means of bitcoin will be a clever monetary move, enlarged institutional agreement could lead to extra applications for normal clients and influence the cost of cryptocurrencies not anything is sure, except if you acquire cryptocurrencies as a long-standing store of worth, the greater the likelihood that demand and value will rise as it finds more "real world" applications.

Upcoming of NFTs

Non-fungible tokens, or NFTs, have existed since 2014, but it wasn't until 2021 that this cutting-edge technology became widely accepted.

NFTs, which stand for digital ownership of a variety of unreplicable intangible goods, have caught the interest of prominent people and large corporations like American Express and Gucci. According to data gathered by DappRadar, an app store for decentralized applications, total NFT sales reached $25 billion in 2021 as opposed to $94.9 million the earlier time.

However, the question of whether NFTs are merely a fad or a trend is still up for debate. According to data from DappRadar, NFT sales declined below $1 billion in June for the first time in the previous 12 months.

The opinions of experts are still divided; some call NFTs a "bubble," while others argue that the smart contracts used in blockchain technology, which underlie them, are what actually provide genuine worth Artists and producers are asserting that this is the newest method of income in the meantime.

What investors should know about the fall in NFTs?

Numerous people purchased NFTs throughout the past year, either as investments or just for enjoyment. Whatever the reason, the recent collapse of the cryptocurrency market has significantly reduced the value of many of those digital assets. You should probably avoid NFTs knowing that they are even riskier and more speculative than crypto, especially as the price of bitcoin is generally declining.

According to experts, most long-term investors will be better off investing in bitcoin or Ethereum, two of the biggest cryptocurrencies, instead of an NFT, with a tiny amount of their portfolio (less than 5%, and never at the expense of achieving other financial goal).

Viewpoint for DeFi

If you contain any cryptocurrency savings, you've almost certainly heard of the saying "DeFi." It stands for "decentralized finance" and alludes to a digital environment where alternative financial services run on blockchain and cryptocurrency technologies. DeFi replaces conventional intermediaries like banks and lenders with "smart contracts." In essence, software is replacing the companies we deal with on a daily basis to handle our accounts. As a result, there is no central authority to which DeFi entities must answer.

DeFi, however, is still in its relative infancy, much like the early days of the internet, when there were few websites, few online services, and primitive chat rooms, giving the impression of the "Wild West." With that in mind, analysts predict that there may be some hiccups along the way with its development, but eventually there may be a Google or Amazon of the DeFi space.

Meaning of increased DeFi use for investors

DeFi is the place to go if you want complete and utter control over your possessions. However, there may be a trade-off because there are fewer legal barriers to protect your assets. In many ways, DeFi resembles the "wild west" of banking and investment, where there may be no way to reclaim your money if you lose them to hackers or through other earnings. DeFi is still in its infancy, so it's wise to balance the dangers and potential rewards when contrasting it with other financial solutions.

Since the DeFi market is unregulated, you'll have to take more financial risks, but you'll also have more freedom and control. To get started, you'll need to have a basic knowledge of cryptography and purchase some cryptocurrency. According to experts, it's ideal to only have 5% of your whole portfolio invested in cryptocurrencies, and only after you've amassed an emergency fund and paid off any high-interest balance

Outlook for Bitcoin's Future

Since it is the most valuable cryptocurrency by market cap and the rest of the market tends to mimic its tendencies, Bitcoin is an excellent predictor of the crypto market as completely. After a tumultuous ride in 2021, the price of bitcoin reached a new record high in November when it surpassed $68,000. But in 2022, it all came tumbling down.

As a result of continuous macroeconomic uncertainties mostly caused by rising prices, Bitcoin and the larger cryptocurrency market have been declining this year. Fears of a recession, rising interest rates, unstable financial markets, and inflation. Since last November, Bitcoin has lost more than two-thirds of its value and recently fell as low as $17,500. On whether bitcoin has bottomed out yet, experts are divided. Some claim it has already happened, while others predict a drop to $10,000 for bitcoin in 2022.

Because of this volatility, experts advise keeping your initial cryptocurrency investments to less than 5% of your overall portfolio. But how far can bitcoin advance over the long run? Despite bitcoin's rough start to the year, analysts continue to predict that it will reach $100,000; it is more a question of when than if.

The history of Bitcoin may offer some hints as to what to anticipate going forward.

Outlook for Ethereum Future

The second-largest cryptocurrency and most well-known alternative coin is called Ethereum. It can be used as a reliable indicator of the cryptocurrency market, much like bitcoin. Its value has increased dramatically over the past six years, rising from $0.311 at its introduction in 2015 to nearly $4,800 at its peak in late 2017.

Despite being some distance from its all-time high, the price of Ethereum has the potential to increase significantly throughout the rest of 2022. According to experts, the outcome of Ethereum's significant upgrade, scheduled for September 19, could affect that figure. Ethereum is updating its technology to a less energy-intensive version known as "The Merge" among insiders.

The network will allegedly become quicker, more affordable, and more effective as a result of the update. Experts predict that ether might once again break $4,000 in 2022 and may even reach $12,000 if Ethereum keeps its promises with the integration. Investors are keeping a close eye on every development leading up to the merger and, in some circumstances, profiting from the present market slump by purchasing the dip in front of it. According to analysts, only time will tell if Etherium's price will rise or drop back to earlier lows.

What the price volatility of bitcoin and Ethereum means for investors

The volatility of bitcoin and Ethereum is another justification for investors to play a steady long fixture, don't be concerned with short-term volatility if you're buying with the intention of long-term growth.

The best course of action is to “set it and forget it” and stops thinking about your cryptocurrency investment. Every time there is a price movement, whether it is up or down, experts continue to warn us that emotional reactions can lead investors to act hastily and make choices that cause them to lose money on their investment.

Cryptocurrency's Future

The reality is that cryptocurrency is still a new and speculative investment with little historical data on which to base predictions. We can guess on what value bitcoin may have for investors in the coming months and years (and many will). No of what a particular expert believes or claims, nobody truly knows. For long-term wealth creation, it is crucial to only invest what you are willing to lose and to stay with more traditional investments.

Keep your investments modest, and never prioritize cryptocurrencies over other financial objectives like retirement savings and debt repayment with high interest rates.

Chapter 4

Industries that Blockchain Will Soon Disrupt

Let's be honest. Many people are reluctant to adopt new technologies in both their personal and professional life. They cannot frequently envision how the new technology they are opposing will enhance their quality of life in the future. New technologies are fascinating because they inspire innovation and create global opportunities. They impact the way we think and act every day, which changes our life. More than only our daily lives can be impacted by technological innovation. It has the power to upend entire industries and alter how we conduct business. Affected industries are compelled to change or face replacement as new technologies are produced.

Blockchain technology is the most recent innovation that is soon becoming the next significant disruption.

A digital ledger technology called blockchain is used to safely record transactions. It has the potential to change how commerce is conducted around the world.

Here are nine well-known sectors that blockchain technology is expected to revolutionize shortly.

1. The Banking Sector

The banking industry now faces numerous key issues that blockchain technology can address. Currently, banks handle both the storage and transfer of money for their clients. Blockchain offers a built-in safety mechanism that would offer long-term records of the daily millions of transactions that occur in the banking sector. By offering secure records, this ledger system might greatly reduce the danger. Furthermore, thanks to blockchain's decentralization, money might be exchanged more quickly and cheaply.

2. The Real land Sector

A real estate transaction involves a significant amount of paperwork, as anyone who has ever bought or sold a home will attest. The current hassle that all of this paperwork generate can be radically changed by blockchain technology. All of the papers and transaction records may be securely preserved utilizing blockchain with significantly less effort and expense.

Smart contracts that only release funding when the requirements are satisfied can be made using the technology. Furthermore, a lot of individuals who are working with real estate agents are aware of how frustrating commission rates can be, with many charging up to 6%.

With its platform that is powered by cryptocurrencies, Deed coin hopes to change that.

These charges are reduced to just 1% by using the Deed coin platform and exclusive tokens. Except for direct transactions between agents and clients, Deedcoin's distributed architecture tokenizes the transaction and cuts out all intermediaries, giving control back to homebuyers and sellers.

3. The Medical Sector

When it comes to exchanging and keeping medical information and data, the healthcare sector has needed a major disruption. Customers and healthcare providers are less trusting of one another as a result of the possibility of error, fraud, and missing records. By securely keeping medical records that can be accurately and securely transferred to and accessed by the doctors and other persons who are permitted, blockchain technology can restructure the trust.

The identification and authorization of people will be facilitated by blockchain. A business by the name of Ontology is already striving to use blockchain technology to make positive, multi-source identification a reality across all industries.

4. The Legal Sector

By having the ability to store and authenticate documents and data, blockchain technology is poised to upend some sectors of the legal sector. For instance, litigation involving addressing issues with decedents' wills or any other papers can be avoided. Wills and other records kept on the blockchain will be confirmed promptly and securely. The papers will be authenticated and stored if they are modified.

Blockchain technology can also resolve any inheritance-related legal disputes, including those involving bitcoin holdings. For instance, Safe Haven offers users the chance to safeguard digital assets so that the investor's legacy can be safely and securely passed down to his children or designee. Long legal fights battling over digital inheritance are eliminated by this technique.

5. The Industry of Cryptocurrency Exchanges

Blockchain makes it possible for digital currency, which is the currency of the future, to be transmitted and recorded safely. But it takes a lot of processing power to "mine," or verify and authenticate, every digital currency transaction. Due to the enormous amount of processing necessary, this has recently caused a lot of problems on several platforms when certain transactions "ran out of gas" or fizzle.

Users were losing significant time and money because of this problem.

The way the bitcoin exchange market operates is changing as a result of recent advancements in blockchain technology. With the development of Zen Protocol, the most important problems in the cryptocurrency industry have been resolved. Unlike other platforms, Zen Protocol uses smart contracts, which are aware of the amount of computing each contract will need in advance. That tells us that the contract won't run unless there is enough "gas" to fund it.

6. Political Sector

Government parties in the United States and other countries have recently come under fire for allegedly rigging elections.

But if blockchain technology is used, voter registration, identification verification, and vote counting would all be taken care of, ensuring that only valid votes were to be counted. Vote recounts and election-day controversy are a thing of the past.

7. The Startup Sector

There is currently no method for the thousands of companies searching for funding to approach the proper investors without endangering the confidentiality of their business plans. There is also no ideal mechanism for investors to locate the businesses they want to support. All of that can be changed by blockchain technology. In actuality, it has already begun. Startups now have a safe way to pitch to investors live thanks to businesses like Pitch Ventures.

Entrepreneurs summarize their goods or services so that investors can look through them quickly and identify prospective business prospects. The pitches can be conducted securely using Ethereum's Smart Contract address, protecting the participants' privacy.

8. The video sector

By 2021, it is expected that video will account for 82% of all Internet traffic, and blockchain might have a big impact by decentralizing the video infrastructure. By utilizing the $30 billion in underutilized Internet computer services, decentralizing video encoding, storage, and content distribution will significantly lower the cost of video traffic. By releasing this cash, startups like VideoCoin are already delivering on their promise, paving the way for the emergence of completely fresh and cutting-edge ecosystems for video apps.

9. The Sector of Education

With the help of a cutting-edge Internet that mixes blockchain, bitcoin, and virtual reality, the education sector is prepared to experience some huge advancements. This brand-new Internet, or "3DInternet," has the potential to establish a truly worldwide classroom. To make this a reality, SocratesCoin is taking significant action. A global community of professors, students, campuses, and curricula will be developed by the company. There will be students from all different ages, backgrounds, and places. Nauka University, which will use the 3DInternet to connect science, thought leadership, and science through education, has been protected by SocratesCoin.

Data can be recorded and transferred in a secure and auditable manner using blockchain distributed ledger technology.

Any industry that uses data or transactions in any manner could be disrupted, and it could change the way we go about our daily lives. And it's fantastic that there is so many disturbances.

Whether you enjoy incorporating new technology into your life or not, I think we can all agree that greater protection for our financial data would increase everyone's sense of safekeeping

Chapter 5

How to Profit from Cryptocurrency

Everyone enters the Bitcoin industry intending to make money, but not everyone succeeds. With the increase in crypto frauds, many people either give up along the route or fall victim to some form of trap Aside from the apparent method of trading, there are quite a few additional ways to use cryptocurrencies to earn genuine income. As a result, we decided to investigate some of the tested methods for using cryptocurrencies to generate income. We discovered quite a few, but be assured that you'll find them to be extremely amazing.

Here are 11 ways to earn money using cryptocurrencies right now, without further ado.

1. Invest and hold

This is the most typical method of using cryptocurrency to make currency. The majority of investors buy cryptocurrencies like Bitcoin, Litecoin, Ethereum, Ripple, and others and wait for their values to increase. They sell for a profit once their market prices increase. Finding more stable and volatile assets that can change in value quickly and produce consistent returns is necessary for this investing strategy. Possessions like Bitcoin and Ethereum contain a record of maintaining reliable price variations; as an effect, they preserve be viewed as protected investments in this logic. However, you are free to sell any item that you believe will increase in value; all you have to do is research every asset you buy before deciding to HODL it.

Additionally, investing in pricey assets is not necessary to benefit. Consider having a mix of all coins that have a promising future value and are not simply well-liked in the exchanges. There are hundreds of minor altcoins that have reasonable price movements.

2. Receive dividends in cryptocurrency

You can purchase cryptocurrencies and hold them for the dividend, did you know that? There are a few coins, nevertheless, that will pay you just for acquiring and holding their digital assets. The best part about these coins, especially when stored in a wallet, is that you don't even have to stake them. COSS, CEFF, NEO, KUCOIN, and other coins are a few instances of those that distribute dividends.

Not all of these coins, like traditional equities, are appropriate for your portfolio; you must study and choose those that appear to be consistent with your investing goal.

3. Run cryptocurrency master nodes

A crypto master node is what?

These are full nodes that encourage the various node operators to carry out their functions in running a blockchain. In other words, a master node is a bitcoin full node or digital wallet that keeps a running log of all transactions on a blockchain. One of the most popular methods of generating passive revenue in this industry is running crypto master nodes. However, how precisely do you profit from this?

Let me...

Numerous cryptocurrencies compensate node operators for keeping an up-to-date log of their transactions on their native blockchains. Since the procedure is complicated and requires one to have a specific minimum amount of coins under their master nodes, cryptocurrency platforms prefer to pay master node operators to provide the service.

DASH and PIVX are two examples of proof-of-stake cryptocurrencies with master nodes.

4. Stake crypto

This is an additional way to make money with cryptocurrencies; it gives a double earning potential through price growth and dividend payments from certain coins in exchange for staking (or "proof-of-stake").

Staking is keeping funds in a live wallet, which enables you to make additional money intended for serving to protect a certain crypto network. NAV Coin, PIVX, Neblio, Decred, and many other coins are a few instances of coins that can be staked.

5. Day Investing

More than 80% of cryptocurrency investors think that day trading is the only practical method to make money in this industry, if not the only way. However, most of them are unaware that day trading entails more than merely keeping an item until its price enlarges; it is complicated to turn out to be a day trader, plus having the essential systematic and technological abilities is critical.

The most demanding although, in my view, one of the most worthwhile ways to make currency through cryptocurrencies is to assess market charts resting on the presentation of the listed asset. Any exchange nowadays allows you to start day trading; all you have to do is sign up, purchase some assets, and conduct some analysis to get started. You can also begin trading using an automated trading platform like bitcoin profit, which enables users to interpret signals sent out by trends on bitcoin and other cryptocurrencies and begin operating as a successful little dealer

6. Assist with Micro tasks involving Cryptocurrency

You can work on little jobs for people or bitcoin sites and earn money if you have additional time. The tasks can be very different; they could involve testing apps, watching advertisements, doing surveys, watching films, and more.

7. Work with Bitcoin-related businesses

This is a typical method of making money in the business anybody can work for a bitcoin business in any capacity; you could, for example, be a digital marketer, content creator, or web designer. All you have to do is determine their needs and demonstrate how your abilities can help them.

The nicest part of working with crypto platforms is that you'll probably do so remotely, giving you the freedom to do so in the comfort of your own home. Other than that, most crypto companies offer appealing packages, so if you can work with any trustworthy ones, seize the chance.

8. Bitcoin Arbitrage

Since the cryptocurrency industry is mostly unregulated, there are many differences in terms of asset valuation, product pricing, and other factors.

The majority of exchanges set their listing prices, which has helped to eliminate differences in asset volatility and liquidity. If carefully considered, buying from inexpensive sources and selling on exorbitant exchanges are two ways to profit from these price discrepancies. Arbitrage is essentially described in this manner.

If you put your act together, you can locate price spreads on several exchanges ranging from 5% to 30%. Consider registering on several sites and comparing asset prices to uncover any appreciable differences to profit from.

10. Bitcoin Faucets

Although they are not particularly well known, cryptocurrency faucets are a very effective way to make cash the most well-known ones are bitcoin faucets, which are essentially a reward system that functions as a website or application and provides incentives to eligible users in the form of Satoshi. A Satoshi is a reward given for accomplishing a task, such as capture, or any other that may be necessary by the application or website. It is equal to one-hundredth of a millionth BTC. The responsibilities could even take the form of enjoyable activities like playing games, watching films, or seeing particular advertisements. You receive a tiny amount of Bitcoin for each assignment you complete. To generate any real money using cryptocurrency faucets, you might need to finish a variety of chores.

11. Produce content about cryptocurrency

One of the most efficient ways to reach out to current or potential customers during the last ten years is through content. The most effective way to launch new goods or services is through content. Because most projects in the cryptocurrency industry are virtual, content marketing plays a significant role in this business Therefore; it might not be able to contact the target population through traditional marketing techniques. You can provide written material, info graphics, or videos for numerous cryptocurrency brands, and this is where the opportunity is.

Add cryptocurrencies to your list of accepted payment options. If you're a business owner, accepting cryptocurrency payments might bring in big profits.

Statistics demonstrate that while few investments reach 100% in years, the market value of various cryptocurrencies has increased by thousands of percentage points in a single day.

The only thing left to do is choose the best payment method to accept cryptocurrency; here is a couple to get you started:

- Coin Box
- The Bit Pay
- Coin Door
- SpectroCoin

Chapter 6

From planning to avoiding FOMO

Even within the longer-term trends known as bull and bear markets, the Bitcoin and cryptocurrency markets have experienced numerous cycles of growth and collapse since their launch in 2009. Although market declines have, so far, been followed by recoveries and strong gains, experienced traders and novice investors alike may find it difficult to manage these times.

Here, we go over five tactics you might wish to employ during a market downturn to preserve the value of your portfolio, stay away from irrational trading decisions, and get more break

1 - Avoid succumbing to FOMO and FUD

Keeping up with the most recent news and trends in the bitcoin industry is essential, but too much knowledge can be harmful. This is especially true during market downturns when it's all too easy to let your emotions take over and place some transactions at the wrong time.

• In the world of cryptocurrencies, the terms "FOMO" and "FUD" are frequently used, and they can have a bigger impact on our buying and selling decisions than many of us would want to admit.

FUD is a term used to describe a bad market mood brought on by a rumor, adverse news report, or a well-known individual voicing concerns about a specific market or asset. As traders sell their shares in anticipation of additional price declines, this may harm the price.

The opposite is FOMO, which describes a trader's propensity to lose sight of fundamental indications in a rush to board the next spacecraft to the moon after seeing encouraging price movement or news. Always keep in mind that no one can foretell the future, and you should never rely on someone else's advice instead of conducting your research and drawing your conclusions. Influencers and publications may occasionally have a financial stake in spreading FUD or FOMO to steer the markets in a particular way. Always try to confirm with several sources while learning about the most recent developments throughout bitcoin marketplaces.

2-Set specific objectives, diversify, and only engage in trading within your means as your second strategy.

You should never invest more money than you can afford to lose, regardless of how sure you are about a certain item. Nobody likes to experience an emotional rollercoaster while watching their portfolio's price progressively decline while hoping for positive price action.

- The majority of astute investors also decide to hold a variety of various assets for an extended period to diversify their portfolio, ranging from alternative cryptocurrencies to stock market index funds.

• The phrase "crypto doesn't sleep" is used frequently. Because the cryptocurrency markets are notoriously volatile, cryptocurrency investors should plan out their trading strategy, including, if at all possible, their entry and exit points.

• Even if you had access to all the information, prices could fall as a result of a black swan occurrence, hack, or tweet from a well-known person. This is why it's so important to prepare in advance and to take action to reduce your losses in the event of a rapid fall.

• Investors might think about using set tactics like dollar-cost averaging, which allows buyers of cryptocurrencies to fully avoid trading on emotion or need to keep their eyes glued to the plan

Keep in mind: When holding volatile assets like cryptocurrencies, it's quite simple to lose control.

Investors should attempt to develop a goal that balances reducing potential losses with obtaining potential gains because trading may be a very high-risk activity, particularly in a negative market.

3: Thinking strategically and long-term

The adage "it's not a loss until you sell" may only be partially accurate, but it still has some merit. Unrealized losses, or decreases in asset value since the acquisition, are only recognized when an asset is sold for less than the original purchase price.

• Throughout the long run, Bitcoin has steadily trended upward over time History demonstrates that prices are likely to recover eventually owing to economic factors like scarcity, regardless of whether prices are declining due to a brief market correction or a more protracted bear market.

Many people think that this restricted supply will lead to a long-term increase in the price of cryptocurrencies like Bitcoin. Negative price movement can be seen as transient if you invest over a longer period (years rather than weeks or months).

• Holding investments over extended periods has so far been a successful tactic, with Bitcoin emerging as conceivably the most successful large asset of the previous ten beings.

Keep in mind that holding cryptocurrencies for extended periods can be advantageous in terms of taxation in nations like the US. For instance, keeping for a year or longer may be preferable to selling quickly.

4 - Prepare yourself to ride out a downturn or grab profits.

Exchanging several of your unstable crypto assets for extra stable assets is one of the safest habits to reduce crypto instability and defend yourself throughout a market dip. In a bull market for cryptocurrencies, this can assist an investor in "lock-in" their balance, lower their risk, and lessen the stress associated with actively managing their portfolio.

• By turning a portion of your portfolio into stable-value assets, you reduce your exposure to price changes while the markets are quiet. Stablecoins like USDC seek to preserve their value at a predetermined price.

• However, keep in mind that selling everything at once, or capitulation, can easily result in cryptocurrency investors losing out if the market unexpectedly recovers.

This is why it's crucial to determine your level of acceptable profit and loss before you find yourself in a situation where you have to make choices quickly.

Keep in mind that many investors now opt to move in and out of solid assets as part of a bigger withdrawal and buy-back plan, which, if the timing is right, can help investors gradually expand their selection It's not simple, though, and even seasoned investors frequently make mistakes in timing their entries and exits. Dollar-cost averaging is an excellent approach to avoid ever attempting to time the market (again, for many investors).

5: Recognize the possibilities

If you know where to look, there are possibilities even when the cryptocurrency markets are declining. Smart investors see a new window of opportunity to purchase their preferred assets at a discount and make a profit whereas others anticipate a cold and dark crypto winter.

• Buying the dip is a common strategy used by traders to enter the market or boost their positions when they feel priced out of prior gains.

• There will still be little peaks and valleys as the market fluctuates, even during a decline. Technical analysts who have practiced trading might benefit from this situation by using their knowledge to forecast these short-term swings and profit from them by buying the lows and selling the highs.

• Another effective tactic for making money during downturns is short selling, which involves wagering that the value of an asset will decline.

• Even in a bear market or downtrend, activities like staking and DeFi yield farming can help level out returns and offer support to ensure that your actual cryptocurrency balance is continuously growing.

• Dollar-cost averaging is effective whether markets are rising or falling if you think an asset will eventually be worth more! In fact, during downturns, you get more cryptocurrency for your cash

Keep in mind that these activities (with DCA probably being the exception) are not for the faint of heart and may even result in substantial losses or at the very least greatly increase the amount of time you spend in front of a screen watching anxious price charts.

Chapter 7

The Best Way to Assess Any Cryptocurrency

Over the past year, cryptocurrency-interested investors have transformed the cryptocurrency business. Bitcoin and Ethereum have served as the starting point for many of these investors. In terms of potential future growth, they are the most valued and have the longest track records. What about investors that want to make a bigger investment? The riskier you may anticipate your investments to become as you delve deeper into cryptocurrencies and less well-known altcoins.

Price and a few other crucial measures, according to experts, can help investors decide which cryptocurrencies have a high chance of success and which ones are more likely to be unsuccessful Investors should also take into account more qualitative aspects, such as who founded a particular cryptocurrency, use cases, what is in its white paper (if it has one), and more, in addition to quantitative factors like price, market value, and trading quantity

Before analyzing the price movement, you should first perform what is known as fundamental research, which entails selecting the appropriate asset for your objectives.

Whether you're buying bitcoin or a fresh token that just appeared. They hold for all investments in cryptocurrencies, but more so for riskier and more recent

Altcoins:

• Limit your portfolio's cryptocurrency investments to 5% or less.

• Only invest in cryptocurrencies what you're willing to lose.

• Before investing in cryptocurrencies, make sure you have an emergency fund, have paid off any high-interest debt, and have a standard retirement plan in place.

• Start with the two most widely used and well-known cryptocurrencies, bitcoin and Ethereum.

Here's a breakdown of how to assess any Cryptocurrency's long-term potential, regardless of your level of experience or interest in moving beyond bitcoin and Ethereum:

Understanding the basics of cryptography

Before carefully examining the technical aspects that influence a Cryptocurrency's market value, you need to have a basic idea of what you're getting into if you're investing in cryptocurrencies for the long term.

Increase your attention to the project itself, the issue it addresses, and the source of the initiative's true worth.

There are a few qualitative aspects that experts advise considering when evaluating potential cryptocurrency investments when you're conducting your study and determining whether to invest in a potential coin:

Social media and the project website

According to experts, it's crucial to take into account a preliminary high-level overview of the plan.

Visit the cryptocurrency project's website and social media pages to learn more about the project, the team, and the community as well as to get a feel of how socially active it is. The website for the project should be user-friendly, and useful, and publicly provide information about the project, the team working on it, as well as its white paper and roadmap.

The Group

A project's likelihood of success or failure can be significantly influenced by the team's reputation and expertise. If the team is not publicly disclosed, that raises suspicion (bitcoin is thc cxception). Additionally, you should consider the team's recent work on projects and prior experience in the cryptocurrency sector. You might want to find out if this is their first project or if they have a track record of creating profitable crypto initiatives, for instance. Observe the project team's executives as well.

Projects with respectable CEOs or collaborations with well-known businesses are also encouraging.

Road Map with White Paper

The project's white paper and road plan are essential for evaluating a coin or token's long-term value as an investor. A strong and well-defined white paper and roadmap are characteristics of a successful crypto project. A road plan assist set prospect on how a cryptocurrency scheme aims to raise and adjust besides its hoped-for achievement and adoption, whereas a white paper provides technical information about its concept to assist you to decide whether it has any validity.

You wish to view a broad timetable with information on the project's advancement on a road map. You should doubt the project's future success and worth if it lacks a defined vision, white paper, and plan.

Big-time investors

Find out if the project has investors already, and if so, who they are. If reputable investment businesses or significant investors have already made investments in the project, that is a positive sign. It indicates that they have done their homework and have faith in the project's long-term viability.

The Locality

The potential of a particular cryptocurrency can be made or broken for many crypto projects thanks to the community that supports it. The initial and ongoing success of the project is greatly influenced by the energy and size of the community, but you should exercise caution when considering this aspect when evaluating a currency or token.

You shouldn't buy in a currency or token-based just on hype and should take the time to become familiar with all the aforementioned elements before putting too much trust in its community because hype can occasionally exceed and even conceal a project's true utility or value. Figuring out what is what and who is who in a crowd may be very difficult, especially if many people are fervently promoting it. Your objective, however subjective, is to determine if the asset is overvalued or undervalued. Your decision over which coins to buy will be influenced by keeping these facts in mind. After you've mastered the fundamentals, you can employ additional technical measurements and indicators as a supplement to assist in guiding your investment choices.

Chapter 8

Stocks vs. Cryptocurrencies: What's the Difference?

A diversified array of assets should be present in a successful investment portfolio. Spreading risk involves investing in a variety of things, including stocks, bonds, properties, and commodities.

Even more speculative investments are possible. It might have been wildcatters drilling for oil throughout the 20th century (and not always finding it). It might have been internet stocks in the 1990s. At the present, cryptocurrencies (also known as crypto). Investors must strike a balance between comfort and risk when deciding between cryptocurrencies and stocks. Investors in digital currencies have experienced volatile price swings.

Although the ups and downs of the stock market can be exhilarating, they are not quite as extreme as those of cryptocurrencies.

To achieve the investor's objectives, it is essential to comprehend the benefits and drawbacks of each asset as well as their place in a portfolio.

Cryptocurrency: What is it?

In the last ten years, cryptocurrency, a relatively new kind of money, has grown in popularity. Some proponents of cryptocurrencies hope it will replace equities and traditional forms of money as the future of finance, while others fear it is too hazardous to function as a full-fledged financial system due to its uncontrolled structure. Since there is no official support for cryptocurrencies, their value is determined by the market.

Digital resource

On distributed, worldwide networks of computers, cryptocurrencies are managed. The word "cryptocurrency" refers to a system of secure encryption that protects data storage and transactions. To obtain access, a cryptocurrency owner must enter a password with at least 16 characters. (Some cryptocurrency owners who forgot their passwords were unable to access their portfolios.)

Even though there are thousands of cryptocurrencies, Bitcoin was the first and is still the most popular, making up about two-thirds of the market capitalization in 2020. The cryptocurrencies Ethereum, Litecoin, PeerCoin, Namecoin, Cardano, and EOS are also well-known.

Downs and ups

With abrupt fluctuations in value over brief intervals, volatility has been a defining feature of cryptocurrencies. A single Bitcoin could be worth up to $65,000 in 2021, ranging from $28,383 to that amount.

Cryptocurrencies, in particular Bitcoin, are said by proponents to be resistant to inflation. There are only 21 million coins that can be made in Bitcoin, hence there is a limited quantity. The inflation that can happen with currencies backed by governments should be curbed as a result. The use of cryptocurrencies as money is growing. Financial transaction platform Square supports cryptocurrency transactions, and more and more businesses now accept cryptocurrency as payment. El Salvador was the first nation to accept Bitcoin as legal money in 2021.

Blockchain

Blockchain, a distributed ledger system that records and tracks cryptocurrency transactions, is the foundation of cryptocurrency. Blockchain uses encryption, a distributed computer network, and user consensus to track transactions. Each transaction's data is maintained in a block that links to those that came before and after it in a chain that is protected by nearly tamper-proof cryptography. The chain's built-in consensus verifies the transactions. Some contend that blockchain technology at its core represents the true worth of cryptocurrencies. As a means of boosting trust and preventing fraud and money laundering, some firms have used blockchain technology for recording transactions performed with traditional currencies.

Automobiles for investing

With Bitcoin prices exceeding $60,000 per coin, purchasing cryptocurrencies as opposed to stocks may seem more expensive. Investors can, however, purchase fractional shares of bitcoin for less cash other vehicles include unregulated entities' bitcoin funds.

When the Securities and Exchange Commission (SEC) approved the trading of an exchange-traded fund (ETF) linked to Bitcoin in 2021, cryptocurrency passed a significant milestone toward legality as a means of investment. The Chicago Mercantile Exchange's Bitcoin futures market price is what the ETF monitors, not the actual worth of Bitcoin. With the approval of American regulators, the authorization enables brokerage firms to enter the cryptocurrency market.

Overview of the stocks

Consider bitcoin against stocks while keeping in mind that equities represent ownership of a portion of a corporation. At the time of its founding, a corporation belongs entirely to its creator. The entrepreneur may sell ownership shares to investors as the business looks to expand. The big business can choose to perform a municipal contribution at some point to sell shares to new shareholders. As an outcome, the corporation can hoist more finances plus early investors can earn their assets. A business can sell more stock even while it is publicly traded. The corporation can raise money by issuing new stock, which lowers the value of the existing shares. Selling additional stock is frequently done to acquire money for expansion, hire staff, boost output, or construct infrastructure.

At annual stockholder meetings, stockholders have the opportunity to vote on the corporate policy as well as the candidates for the board of directors. They often have limited influence on a company's day-to-day operations, but if enough investors band together, they may be able to influence the company's course.

Creating value

When a stock's value increases, which may happen as a result of a company's performance, investors win. The more a company's stock should climb the more sales and profits it generates. A stock's price might increase even on the promise of improved company performance. In contrast, the investment loses value when the stock price declines as a result of subpar corporate performance or a challenging economic situation

If the business provides dividends, investors also profit from their investments. If a company's board of directors decides that earnings can be distributed, it may start paying dividends; if further capital is required for the firm, it may cut or stop paying dividends. Dividends made every quarter allow a corporation to distribute its profits to shareholders. In general, companies that are more established, older, and have consistent revenue sources are more likely to pay dividends. Younger, rapidly expanding businesses may choose to reinvest profits rather than pay dividends.

Categories of stock

Owners of stock may have regular or preferred shares. Preferred shares get their name from the fact that they occasionally treat stockholders preferentially. For instance, preferred shareholders receive dividends first and at a greater rate of payment.

They receive rewards in advance from owners of common shares in the event of a firm liquidation. However, holders of preferred shares are not entitled to the same voting privileges as holders of common shares.

Depending on their investment objectives, investors can choose to purchase common or preferred shares.

The main distinctions between stocks and cryptocurrencies

While both stocks and cryptocurrencies are respectable investing options, their functions within a portfolio vary. The way they are purchased plus sold, in addition to how they maintain an investing plan, vary radically. Here are a few vital qualities of stocks and cryptocurrencies:

Possession

A purchaser frequently needs to open a bank account at a brokerage like Charles Schwab, TD Waterhouse, or Fidelity in sequence to buy in addition to keeping hold of stock. In the buyer's name, the brokerage executes deals plus holds stock. Even though newer companies like Robinhood have cut down the procedure, their creative contributions aren't as wide. A consumer ought to as well supply individual information similar to their road address plus communal safety digit. A certain stage of safety is provided by utilizing a brokerage.

The theoretical secrecy of crypto is one of its compensation. The individuality of the cryptocurrency buyer is unrelated. A cryptocurrency holder keeps their assets on a USB drive or in a digital wallet.

The disadvantage of mystery is that the lumber of sanctuary rests by way of the owner, who has to memorize a secret word with a minimum of 16 lettering in addition to maintaining track of anywhere the crypto is at all times. If hackers drain owners' cryptocurrency wallets, there isn't a lot they know how to accomplish.

Exchanges

Qualified exchanges around the globe for tender stock trading. They offer safekeeping, constancy, plus simplicity to stock buyers and are intended to handle important daily trading volumes. even though details contrast through the area, exchanges are extremely forbidden, shielding equally buyers and sellers.

Exchanges that allow users to acquire as well as sell cryptocurrencies are further current. There are dozens, if not hundreds, of crypto exchanges.

The two largest are Coinbase and Binance. Some exchanges collaborate with outside organizations to make it simple to convert fiat money, like the dollar, into cryptocurrencies.

Instability

Stock value fluctuations that happen unexpectedly and speedily are as old as stock exchanges. Encouraging reports can increase a stock's value, at the same time as unhelpful information might force it down. Stock markets can break down in a day, as "Black Friday" and "Black Monday" attests. Typically, there is a technical or financial reason (such as a program-driven sell-off). The rate of investors' portfolios can turn down; however, total losses are rare.

Unpredictability is one object cryptocurrencies contain a status designed for. For example, Ethereum began 2021 at about $730 with amplified to $4,080 through the conclusion of May. In July, it was about $1,786, and after that in late October, it was $4,082.

Regulation

The United States recognized the Securities and Exchange Commission (SEC) to make plus support investor safeguards in the wake of the 1929 stock market disaster that sparked the Great misery. Companies have to reveal all details that might affect the value of their shares. There is the prosperity of information accessible intended for investors moreover their financial advisors to employ whilst making investment decisions.

The fact that cryptocurrencies are still mostly unregulated, in contrast, is seen favorably by some crypto investors. Cryptocurrency marketplaces include no regard for national limitations or governmental power. Nevertheless, if something goes incorrect with their investment, it leaves cryptocurrency customers with no safety.

Strategic additions

Both cryptocurrencies and equities have considerable distinctions as well as some commonalities. They can be used in identical folders intended for a variety of purposes through investment professionals who are conscious of their strengths with shortcomings.

Stocks bid safety. For the mainly of the 20th century in addition to into the 21st, they were the chosen investment to boost assets for equally folks with business.

Cryptocurrency investment is riskier. Big returns could be possible, but the danger is larger. They can come together to handle threats in addition to returns within a portfolio of investments.

Chapter 9

How Does NFT Work? And What Is NFT?

Describe NFT

In contrast to non-fungible assets tokens, which are distinct digital assets whose ownership can be monitored on NFT blockchain developments like Ethereum, fungible assets or fungibility refers to an item or an asset that has the potential to trade or get exchanged with a comparable type of asset or thing.

Non-Fungible Tokens, also known as NFTs, are digital assets, a kind of digital certificate for ownership of commodities, or an asset that symbolizes a wide range of tangible and intangible products, including artworks, virtual properties, postcards, films, and so on.

NFTs cannot be duplicated or compared to a similar asset because each non-fungible token asset is distinct in its own right. More information regarding the growth and price of the NFT market can be found here. Let's use a game ticket as an example to help you understand. You would take a baseball game ticket if it were given to you. Right? Will you accept the movie ticket if that person gives it to you in return?

The response: No, you won't, because a movie ticket will not be worth the same as a ticket to a baseball sport. If this example is used in place of an NFT, then the game ticket (which is an NFT) cannot be exchanged for another ticket because each ticket for a baseball game has a distinct uniqueness

The same is true for NFT, where you cannot simply exchange or trade NFT tokens with equal value tokens because each token is unique and has a limited supply.

Examples of Non-Fungible Tokens

Possessing a digital collectible has advantages over real items like rare coins or stamps. Each NFT is made up of distinct information that sets it from other NFTs and makes it simpler to confirm an item's validity.

For instance, because the genuine object can be easily linked to its legitimate user, it renders the circulation of imitation artifacts pointless for artists. Additionally, unlike other NFT crypto coins, you cannot directly exchange NFTs with anyone for the same reason that all NFTs are non-identical or distinct. For instance, even if you have two NFCs on the same platform that are the same size, color, and part of the collection, they still won't be identical. Let's look at a few NFT project examples:

Blockchain Heroes is a unique trading card set that emphasizes the shared traits of individuals in the blockchain and cryptocurrency industries.

Decentraland: In this game, users' virtual worlds can be purchased by gamers. The virtual space's owner can make money from their environment by adding shops, advertisements, etc.

Prospectors.io is a blockchain-based game where participants receive their owned assets in the form of a blockchain and are rewarded with NFT based on their participation.

Gods Unchained is a digital collectible card game or online collecting card game in which the cards are available as free-to-buy and free-to-sell NFTs.

A well-known NFT game that involves breeding and collecting cats is called CryptoKitties. Each of these digital cats' unique "attributes" propelled NFTs into the public eye.

How and Why Did NFT Begin? It's History

There are some disputes around the debut of NFTs. The earliest NFTs are thought to have been colored coins. On the blockchain, colored coins represent real-world goods. Early in 2012, Yoni Assia wrote a blog post titled "bitcoin 2. X (aka Colored Bitcoin) first specs," which is where Colored Coins were first mentioned. According to rumors, Colored Coins encouraged experimentation and created the framework for NFTs.

Following the trade of Rare Pepes on Ethereum, Crypto Punks, the first-ever NFT Token ever created, was eventually launched.

After that, a company by the name of Rare Bits formed as a platform for trading and exchanging NFTs and raised $6 million in funding. A collectible card game known as Gamedex, which raised more than $800,000 in its first few days thanks to the NFTs' mindset, was made possible. Currently, American digital artist Beeple debuted his piece titled "Every day. The First 5000 Days," which sold for $69 million (42329.453 ETH). One of the first NFT-equipped works of art to be listed in some of the top auction houses.

A recent agreement between the NBA and Dapper Labs also saw the beta release of NBA TopShot Collectible and Tradable NFT-based apps. This has been in development since 2018 and will be released in the first half of 2020. The collection consists of packs of tokens that include data and multimedia mashed together.

The Cause of NFT's Recent Popularity

The NFTs have been employed in a variety of businesses throughout the years, and they are now frequently referred to as Ethereum Tokens based on ERC-721. NFTs are now well-liked due to several incredible features:

• Since the entire NFT database is securely recorded in the blockchain, tokens can never be lost, destroyed, or duplicated under any conditions

• The scarcity of NFTs is the primary source of value for them. Although NFT developers can create a limitless amount of tokens, this is done on purpose to preserve their value.

• NFTs cannot be broken into smaller denominations like Bitcoins since they are completely indivisible.

• NFTs can be easily traced to their true owner thanks to the capabilities of blockchain, which also permanently eliminates the need for third-party verification.

Fun Fact because they are fungible, bitcoins can be traded while still holding their original worth. Unlike conventional cryptocurrencies like Monero, Ethereum, and Bitcoin, NFTs cannot be directly swapped with another person.

What Are the Characteristics of Distant Non-Fungible Tokens?

1. Not Compatible

The information stored in NFTs cannot be transmitted or used in any other way since they adhere to the ERC-721 standard, making them non-interoperable.

2. Rare

NFTs are now relatively rare and present in very small numbers worldwide. Because of their rarity and great worth, they are both uncommon and valuable. Simply put, NFs will be more expensive the less there are.

3. Unbreakable

Blockchain is used to handle and store NFTs, which increases their level of security. As a result, they cannot ever be eliminated or deleted.

4. Divergent

Because NFT crypto coins are non-fungible and have an arbitrary value, you can't send them to anyone in part (unlike other cryptocurrencies). One bitcoin, for instance, will remain worth the same after a transfer, but NFT won't.

5. Special

NFTs use blockchain to differentiate themselves from the competition and establish the veracity of a piece of art by resonating with actual works of art. You can also use it to tell authentic products from their replicas.

The NFTs' Working Methodology

NFTs are distinct cryptocurrency tokens controlled by a blockchain. Since each NFT contains a code, a unique ID, and other metadata that no other token can match, the blockchain serves as the decentralized ledger that tracks its ownership and transaction history.

The functioning of non-fungible tokens Let's read the following to find the answer:

NFT creation can be carried out through contract-enabled blockchains with the use of the proper resources and assistance.

EOS, NEO, and now NFT standards are all included in Ethereum, one of the first widely utilized cryptocurrencies. The coins' smart contracts enable the addition of specific information, such as the identity of the owner, among other things.

When combined with digital media, this approach gives NFTs the features of scarcity and royalty that make them appealing:

Scarcity

When we discuss scarcity, we mean that the owner has the discretion to determine whether an asset is scarce. For instance, the owner of the venue selects how many tickets will be sold for each given sporting event or performance. Similar to the NFT token market, the inventor can choose how many copies to make. As a result, each of these copies differs somewhat from the others.

Another illustration of how to generate non-fungible tokens shows that the creator can only create one NFT token, making it a unique, uncommon item. In any event, every NFT will have a distinctive identity, such as a bar code on each piece of clothing or ticket that may appear to be similar but is distinctively different.

Royalties

NFTs are created using computer code known as "smart contracts," which regulates aspects like managing transferability and confirming ownership. Additionally, NFTs can be configured to provide features and functions beyond fundamental ownership and transferability, much like any software program (which also involves the linking of NFT to other digital assets).

As an illustration, a smart contract may be written so that some NFTs automatically distribute a portion of the price received for any sale of the NFT, effectively paying royalties to the original owner.

An NFT is created when someone writes the smart agreement code that controls the non-fungible tokens' properties and adds them to the blockchain where the NFT is proscribed NFTs can be handled by a variety of blockchains, such as Ethereum (with its well-known ERC-721 and ERC-1155 smart contract principles), Flow chain, and Wax, all of which employ comparable measures Because some NFT markets work with specific blockchains, choosing the right blockchain for NFT might have serious consequences for the seller if the right choices are not prepared

Use Cases for Non-Fungible Tokens in Different Industries

1. Gaming

The majority of games have virtual money built into their environment that facilitates player growth. Having said that, accounts with a large number of acquired commodities are in high demand in a market that is uncontrolled and constantly growing. Players will be able to quickly exchange in-game collectibles with sufficient validation and security thanks to the various uses of NFTs.

2. Electronic assets

NFTs are unquestionably the ideal solution for digital assets including house plans, mock-ups, themes, and domains.

Additionally, the virtual property is becoming increasingly common in modern games like Decentral Land. They enable gamers to acquire and create a collection of areas in a virtual environment. The incorporation of NFT can ensure that these things' original producers can be identified.

3. Theft of identity.

NFTs can be used to stop identity theft for items that reflect the identity and can be digitalized, such as medical records and academic credentials. Additionally, the value of non-fungible tokens is demonstrated by the fact that digital artists can use them to convert their creations and secure exclusive copyright for them. Additionally, it aids in distinguishing genuine goods from fakes.

4. Digital Artifacts

NFTs are uncommon and are mostly used in art and collectibles. The presence of this token makes it simple to confirm the ownership and authenticity of a collectible or work of art. Additionally, it enables an artist to stop the theft or piracy of their creations. The use of NFT in cards and items has already begun.

5. Labeling and Certification

NFTs have a specific collection of data about a good or asset loaded into them. They are thus the ideal choice for distributing credentials, credentials, identities, and licenses. To make the identification or certification traceable back to the source, it can be immediately issued through the blockchain as an NFT.

When the NFT concepts are understood, the advantages of a blockchain with smart contracts that may be a powerful force for change are readily apparent.

Benefits of Non-Fungible Tokens

Property Rights

Non-fungible token advantages can be used to handle unusual issues in both the virtual and physical worlds. This has been used for games and collectibles in the digital world (to prove someone owns a specific CryptoKitty or object), but it might also be used for rare items in the real world, like houses, cars, works of art, or even people. Additionally, it might be used to grant restricted access, such as access to Airbnb during specified times or for airline tickets.

Customization Strategy

Benefits of Unlike other tokens that cannot be, non-fungible tokens are secure. Some of the functions of non-fungible tokens may be performed by smart contracts and fungible tokens. The information is all held by the token itself in the non-fungible token market, though.

The token may also have additional information assigned to it, such as its name and owner, as well as information about its past and related information, such as a picture of the house the token represents, a list of the vehicle's previous owners, or the number of character skins available in a game with a similar model type.

Fair Trade

In general, the value of non-fungible tokens may be seen in the fact that it might be difficult or even prohibited at times to transfer ownership of real or digital things because of the risk of fraud. It would be considerably simpler and more efficient to exchange anything addressed by the token thanks to the security of blockchain technology and the distinctiveness of non-fungible tokens. As a result, it might make it possible to transfer ownership of products between platforms or even make them interoperable with other services like games or NFT marketplaces.

When it comes to the traits of NFT, there is a wide range of traits. It is necessary to weigh the risks associated with each advantage to demonstrate it.

The dangers of NFT valuations

If you're wondering how to purchase NFT, Then you should be aware that buying an NFT is a dangerous option given that its value is expected to rise, just like buying any collection. NFTs are a developing industry, thus there is no assurance that there will be the same level of demand for digital assets as there is for Blockchain asset tokenization trading cards or purchasing a real asset. You risk paying a hefty sum for an NFT that loses value over time or is impossible to sell if there is no market for it. You could even create your own NFT, but there is no guarantee that anyone will buy it, so you risk wasting your time and wealth

Storage

Blockchain technology is used to record sales in NFT, proving ownership. Through marketplaces and platforms like Open Sea or Raible, real NFTs are created and kept.

There is no guarantee that you would have the ability to access the work if these sites were to go down for any reason. This renders it less secure than real works of art that hang on walls, gaming tickets, or collectible playing cards.

Regulation

NFTs are not regulated; hence a great deal of confidence is needed. If you don't think the NFT you're buying is a genuine original work of art that hasn't been copied from somewhere else, you might run into copyright problems.

Additionally, there may be platform crackdowns and restrictions on how much collectors can contribute if administrators and authorities get concerned about this booming business This can result in a decline in the market value of NFT tokens.

The Hot-Pot Effect

There may be a "hot potato" effect with NFT games. In other words, players purchase an asset intending to sell it for a profit, but a market crash could result in a significant loss. For instance, let's say you have a gaming sword that you'd like to sell for more money than you originally paid. The point is, as long as there is a buyer, you will make a profit; however, if there is no buyer for the non-fungible asset or if the market crashes, you will lose funds

Upcoming of NFTs

Despite the dangers, the market for NFTs is expected to reach a record-breaking $100 million by the end of July 2020. Even 40% of new crypto users, according to experts in the field, may start with NFTs.

It is clear that the NFT field is positioned to experience exponential growth in the days to come given that the decentralized finance sector has surpassed a $4 billion assessment

Chapter 10

9 typical cryptocurrency fraud schemes in 2022

Digital currency is a type of money that is kept in a digital wallet and may be converted into actual cash by the owner by transferring it to a bank account. Digital currency is different from cryptocurrencies like bitcoin. Since it runs outside of financial institutions and uses blockchain for verification, it is more difficult to recoup from theft.

Even if bitcoin is a more recent trend, crooks are still stealing via traditional means.

Here are a few typical bitcoin scams to be aware of.

1. Investment strategies using bitcoin

Scammers approach participants in bitcoin investment schemes under the pretense of being seasoned "investment managers." As part of the scam, the so-called investment managers make extravagant claims about their success investing in cryptocurrencies and assure their victims that their investments will be beneficial. The con artists demand payment up front to begin. The crooks then simply steal the upfront payments rather than make cash To access someone's cryptocurrency, the con artists may also ask for personal identity information under the pretense that they need it to transfer or deposit funds.

The use of false famous person endorsement is a diverse type of venture cheat.

To make it seem as though the celebrity is endorsing a significant financial advantage from the investment, scammers acquire real images and lay over them on fake accounts, marketing, or articles. These assertions come from sources that seem credible because they use well-known brand names like ABC or CBS and have polished websites and logos. But the endorsement is a fraud.

2. Rug-pulling fraud

In rug pull scams, fraudsters "pump up" a new project, nonfungible token (NFT), or coin to attract investors. The con artists simply vanish with the money after obtaining it. These investments' software forbids everybody from advertising bitcoin after buying it, leaving them with a valueless investment. The Squid coin cheat, which took its name from the popular Netflix comedy Squid Game, is a general variant of this trick.

To earn cryptocurrency, investors had to play: People would purchase tokens for online games and later earn more to trade for other cryptocurrencies. The price of the Squid token rose from being worth 1 cent to over $90 per token. Trading eventually ceased, and the funds vanished. As users tried to sell their tokens but were unsuccessful, the token value eventually fell to zero. Over $3 million was obtained from these investors by the con artists.

Rug pull scams are also prevalent for NFTs, unique digital assets.

3. Love frauds

Cryptocurrency scams are not new to dating apps. These frauds involve relationships that are established gradually over time, usually through long distances and only online communication. One party regularly persuades the other to offer or pay for funds in cryptocurrency.

Once they contain your funds, the dating scammer vanishes. These frauds are additionally known as "pig slaughtering frauds."

4. Phishing rip-offs

Although they have been around for a while, phishing schemes are still widely used. Scammers send emails with malicious links to bogus websites to collect personal information, such as the private key for a bitcoin wallet. Users of digital wallets only receive a single, unique private key, unlike passwords. However, it is difficult to replace a stolen private key. because every key is limited to a wallet, a new wallet has to be ready in turn to transform this key.

Never enter secure information from an email link to protect yourself against phishing schemes.

No matter how trustworthy the website or link looks to be, always go directly to the page.

5. Attack by a man in the middle

Scammers can access bitcoin users' private information when they log in from a public place. Some information exchanged over a communal system, together with passwords, bitcoin wallet keys, plus account information, is vulnerable to interception by scammers.

A hacker knows how to get this secret information after a user is logged in by employing a man-in-the-middle attack approach. When trusted networks are close by, Wi-Fi signals from individual networks are intercepted. Utilizing a virtual private network to block the middleman is the most effective defense against these assaults (VPN).

All data being transmitted is encrypted via the VPN, preventing hackers from accessing personal data and stealing cryptocurrency.

6. Scams involving cryptocurrency giveaways on social media

Social media sites are flooded with fake posts that advertise bitcoin giveaways. To entice consumers, some of these scams also use phony celebrity accounts to promote the offer. Nevertheless, when a user clicks on the advertising, they are transferred to a fake website that desires confirmation in turn to send them bitcoin. Making payment as part of the verification process demonstrates the legitimacy of the account.

The victim runs the threat of losing this reimbursement otherwise, still bad, clicking on a malicious link results in the theft of their data and bitcoin.

7. Ponzi schemes.

Ponzi schemes pay their older investors out of the earnings of new investors. Bitcoin will be used by cryptocurrency crooks to attract fresh investors. Since there are no reliable investments, the strategy is a money-making scheme that goes in circles. The pledge of vast riches with tiny menace is the central attraction of a Ponzi scheme. Nonetheless, there are always dangers connected to these investments, and no earnings can be certain.

8. Fake exchanges for cryptocurrencies

Scammers might entice investors with claims of a fantastic cryptocurrency exchange or even extra bitcoin. However, there isn't an exchange, and the investor doesn't realize it's a scam until they've already lost their riches.

To keep away from an unknown exchange, stick to renowned cryptocurrency exchange marketplaces like Coinbase, Crypto.com, and Cash App. Before entering any personal information, do some research and look for information on the exchange's reputation and legitimacy on industry websites.

9. Job offers and dishonest staff

To gain access to bitcoin accounts, scammers will often pretend to be recruiters or job searchers. Using this scam, they offer a forceful profession at the same time as demanding cryptocurrency in exchange for work training. Scams connecting the use of remote workers live also. For example, North Korean IT freelancers are attempting to take advantage of remote job opportunities by putting up outstanding resumes and stating that they are based in the United state.

The North Korean fraud that targets cryptocurrency companies was alerted to by the US Department of the Treasury.

These independent IT contractors look for work involving virtual currency and make use of access to currency exchangers. To raise funds or steal information for the Democratic People's Republic of Korea, they then hack into the systems (DPRK). These individuals also carry out other professional IT tasks and employ their insider access to enable hostile cyber attacks by the DPRK.

How to safeguard cryptocurrencies like bitcoin

Here are some of the typical warning signs of bitcoin scams:

• Guarantees of significant profits or doubling the investment;

- Only recognizing payments in cryptocurrencies;
- Contractual responsibilities;
- Spelling and grammar mistakes in emails, posts on social media, or any other type of communication;
- Psychological tricks like extortion or blackmail;
- Free money promises;
- Phony celebrity endorsements or influencers who look out of place;
- Only a few details regarding the investment and money transfer; and
- Many transactions in a single day.

Practice excellent digital security habits like using strong passwords only on secured connections or VPNs, and selecting safe storage to defend digital wallets from scammers.

Wallets appear in double varieties: hardware in addition to digital. Because they are housed online, digital wallets are more likely to be compromised. Hardware wallets enable offline storage of data on a device, including the bitcoin wallet and keys. Keeping cryptocurrency safe is necessary since it is not covered by the Federal Deposit Insurance Corporation. No account discloses access codes or wallet keys to any person.

Conclusion

One of the biggest obstacles for investors when it comes to cryptocurrencies is not falling victim to the hype. Investors are still being advised by analysts to beware of cryptocurrencies' high volatility and unpredictable nature. Similar to any other investment, doing your research is crucial if you've decided to invest in the bitcoin market. To better assess whether this kind of investment opportunity is useful for you, think about why you are interested in this particular investment vehicle and educate yourself on cryptocurrencies and blockchain technology.

www.ingramcontent.com/pod-product-compliance
Lightning Source LLC
LaVergne TN
LVHW010605160826
845677LV00013B/3245

* 9 7 9 8 8 4 8 8 3 5 7 0 0 *